glitching

♦

stu hatton

Stu Hatton is a Melbourne-based poet and freelance editor. He works as a mental health researcher at the University of Melbourne. His first collection of poems, *How to be Hungry*, was published in 2010 by (outer) publishing.

glitching

♦

stu hatton

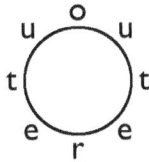

(outer) publishing

First printing: 2014

Published by (outer) publishing
Melbourne, Australia

outerblog.tumblr.com

www.stuhatton.net

National Library of Australia Cataloguing-in-Publication entry:

Hatton, Stu

glitching

ISBN 978-0-992-44540-9 (pbk.)

A821.3

for Mark

acknowledgements

Thank you to Monica, Arthur, Mum, Dad, Mark, Kam, Bob, Jan and all my family in Australia, the UK and elsewhere. Without your love and support this book would never have been completed.

I'd like to thank all my teachers and students over the years for teaching me to pay attention.

Special thanks to Paul Fearne and Matt Hetherington for helpful advice on the manuscript, as well as initiative and good humour.

Special thanks also to Rory O'Donnell for permission to use the cover image, and for assistance with the cover design.

For advice, encouragement, inspiration, friendship and beautiful gestures along the way (or just for paying attention), thank you to: Phil Airey, Ali Alizadeh, Ivy Alvarez, Chris Andrews, Louis Armand, Kim Asher, Brad Axiak, Daniel Barker, Stuart Barnes, David Beattie, Kristen Bissaillon, Amanda Bolleter, Michelle Cahill, Elizabeth Campbell, Natalie Campbell, Jill Chan, Anne-Marie Christensen, Tom Clark, Chris Clarke, Maxine Beneba Clarke, Steve Cornell, Michael Crane, Toby Davidson, Lisa Dempster, Konstancja Densley, Dhammaruwan, Bhikkhu Dhammasiha, Hayley Elliott-Ryan, Michael Farrell, Kat Flanagan, Sarah Flattley, Wendy Fleming, Adam Ford, Geoff Fox, Robin Freeman, David Gilbey, Linda Godfrey, Steve Grimwade, Kris Hemensley, Vijay Henderson, Kyah Horrocks, Duncan Hose, Bronwen Hyde, Andy Jackson, Mark William Jackson, Katya Johanson, Tiggy Johnson, Jill Jones, Rachel Kendall, Steve Knox, Ray Lam, Klare Lanson, Karen Le Rossignol, Kat Lozan, Kent MacCarter, Richard Macumber, Alexia Maddox, Carmen Main, Jo Marston, Dana Guthrie Martin, Steve McDonald, Sally McPhee, Bronwyn Mehan, Peter Minter, Cayt Mirra, Nathan Moore, Derek Motion, Jal Nicholl, Ed Ng, π.O., Ella O'Keefe, Alec Patric, David Prater, Justin Presser, Michael Reynolds, Judith Rodriguez, Aden Rolfe, Philip Salom, Jo Scicluna, Michele Seminara, Anjan Sen, Fee Sievers, Ben Smith, Marcus Smith, Odette Snellen, Laura Soding, Mariana Soffer, Raz Solo, David Starr, Yarni Stephens, Emily Stewart, Lesley Synge, Daphanie Teo, Charles Thermos, Christine Thompson, Vanessa Toholka, Des Trammachi, John Tranter, Erik van Keulen, Bill Wallace, Chris Wallace-Crabbe, Lisa Wardle, Jessica Wilkinson, Tim Wright, Mark Young, Mikey Young.

Thank you to those of you who allowed your work to be adapted or remixed (as detailed in the notes at the back of the book). Thank you to all my colleagues at Deakin and Melbourne Uni. And of course, apologies to anyone I've forgotten!

contents

entrances

amor fati   3
vow   4
no better hold   5
art in the age of digital reproduction   7
weft   8

detours

amsterdam   11
avignon   12
syd   13
down south   15
the 6-star experience   16
bud   17
sands   18
zero summer   19

glitching

want   23
moral highchair   24
[? are you a numb]   25
sleeper   26
greyscale   27
every amateur hour   28

wasted

deleted scenes   31
sunday   32
meds   33
virus   35
post-   36
outrovert   37
psychopathologies   39
melt   41

md & k   42
impair   43
desist   44
slippages (undead)   46

couplings
coupling   51
dote   52
from suite (sour remix)   53

futures
tame   57
the national conversation   58
otherwise   59
departures, arrivals   61

midways
refuse   65
a book of buddhist monks   66
clair   68
seven concentrations   69
self-help   71
waterclock   72
nightside   73
positive poem   74
flows   75

soil
city soil   79
vectors   81
morn   83
apropos (celebration instructions remix)   84

entheogen
fractalina   89
latent spacejunk   90
music may be older than language   91

entheogen   92
cartouche (sands of the desert remix)   93

exits
after reverdy   97
the optimist   98
rims   101
a dead boy   103
poem   104

notes   106

publication credits   108

entrances

amor fati

'begin anywhere'

working backwards from
                 this low
        (for example)

no matter how dumped,
        how misty
you appear in profile

expect some
through-thought
                 will arrive

a shuttle/shifter,
                        e.g.:
'let's go somewhere
crowded, *I feel*
   like a lot of people'

*

dropper,
drop through the city

nameless,
nearing no completion

'nothing I would
        or would not change' (?)
in this weave,
   this fabric

vow

only way to face this:
                           approach it:

      as poem:

        a making-out:
                making-in:

            into:

no better hold
(a dialogue)

So, allow me to mis-
understand you. I like to

misunderstand. **I know,**
but ... ? Who wants to arrive

at the weight
of all things (or

even close to ...)? Who
wants to *arrive*? **But**

anyway. Why tame
such a mind, why

tame a
mind? **This.**

Why
send search parties

round the reaches
of a lamp,

secrets guarded by
the light? **And?** They said

they held the clearing,
held the better hold. **Oh?**

Why hold a stake
in such answers, in

answers? Neither clutch
nor be clutched.

That. Too long to wait
in that other life.

art in the age of digital reproduction

though who uses anything
for its intended purpose?

a poem may be fluked?

graffiti on t-shirt / speed
of its questions

'i like this intrusion'
(quips the milquetoast / lost
in customer service country)

'killing with kindness': the phrase
becomes a regular

those still bossing bones
the old way

beneath mesh
of q & a, demography, i.d. burial

how to 'decouple' mind, shut
off audio … dissolve?

think a shut eye = sleep?

detector vans roam
counterfeit nighttimes

&/or
wrapper-rustle in abandoned cinema
kindles warm front
in Wernicke's area

weft

tracking in / not yet
scouting for doubts
at sub- checkpoints
of the woven / the
liquid (the woven
liquid?) caretakes a
little detail / a pixel
fetches a trace (who
is it , sucking your
pixel ?) / gathering
tethered inputs to
rearray the flows /
all borders porous

detours

amsterdam

on canal floats DJs
mix genders fleshy
grins streamers the
pink drink for free at
pride parade: 'Prik
Power' (little self-
conscious holding
the can could be
the weed thinking
(feel thinking's such
a feeling Van Gogh
such a seer galleries
as headshops (coffee-
shoppers did you
ever see the night
watch itself disem-
bodied like in-game
nulltime stoned to
the point of not
escaping red light
district which took
so long to find (your
mother bites the 'dam
off as dirty though
questions of trans-
parency (who wants
to be seen to be
free (via Vondelpark
caught the last wave
of shrooms back to
the trees where we
fell back and back
(the reign of the
bicycle cult

avignon

In the *boulangerie*, bought as much as my schoolboy French could
carry.

Paper city: festival posters flooding every surface.

Le Bar Américain screening Wimbledon on an outdoor Bravia.

Table service ought to be sporadic, selective (show of authenticity).

Churches' convenient distances (how many within bell-shot?).

'Only of limited interest to non-Catholics, perhaps' was not what it
said in the visitors' guide.

The phrasebook gets us as far as the laundromat.

Tourist argues with girl-behind-the-desk: surely a half-hour gallery
should advertise as such(!)

Striding, intent on the next photo ... gatecrash a raincoat group-
portrait.

Grey sky hoods the garden.

I don't know a word.

syd

overw
eight s
tubble
d dow
n too m
any on
e-ways
glitter
harbo
red a r
ing tra
fficking
dags in
noted p
ark be
at head
offices i
n shape
of head
aches +
we arg
ue hom
e throu
gh a bir
d-show
openin
g or wh
arf chri
stening
champ
agne co
uture r
ecepto
rs insta

nt by in
stant r
estylin
g stimu
li while
hopefu
ls in a g
rungy y
acht su
ck lips

down south

Mangrove salts. Beachside bins reek of prawn-shell traces. Resorts polish ecstasy down to a fine star. Pour a flagship red, then another. Kids're bred tough here, bob through churns of surf ... while cocky, ageing rubbernecks get dumped, spat, graze-limbed. Beachgoers step through gazes; some sunbaker perves through chinks in the straw hat that roofs his face from the noon. Chopper hovers, spreads concentrics over ocean, sounds the shark alarm. Up the bluff there's a cave of bone, which might be called the skull. For 'those who forget to leave', read 'those who turn to sand'.

Yallingup, Western Australia.

the 6-star experience

The world there for your enjoyment. The steward warned us not to eat the lobsters the islanders were known to offer, but a lot of passengers did regardless ($15 each!). The natives were said to speak 'a deceptive English', adapted for their own ends. The beach was 'untouched', water lucent blues, electrics, turquoise. Palms like pop-ups from a glossed-up brochure. Having the sky to oneself. Today's highlights on the liner: kids' pilates in the gym, gift-wrapping work-shop, guest talk on unlocking your inner chartered accountant. The couple lamented that it would've been lovely to laze on the beach and sip champagne; within ten minutes they were told their day-boat and crew were waiting to take them ashore. Everything included in the price—except gambling in the casino ('naturally'). If we don't have it on board, it is yet to be discovered by Western Civilisation. Western Civilisation, meanwhile, was last CCTVed sporting a Donald Duck mask, exiting a bank. The cruise takes in many beaches, or else the one on deck 14 is open daily, sunrise to sunset. Stewards are always here to assist you, but in the event of an emergency, please press your portable panic buzzer for service (we recommend keeping this on your person at all times, using the lanyard provided).

bud

Have history with you,
makes it hard to be
with you when I am. It's
so beautiful outside, but
outside of what? Hey
now the sun is mighty
loud. Birds call me out,
heavy on the roofs. A
garden disciplined
beyond recognition.
Sidestepping trenches
& amber barrier mesh.
Just another castle keep
under construction: slick,
redolent of quietus. The
walled-in lawns. As if
some fresh, wild ice-comet
might bud in the suburbs.

sands

Sweat behind the knees; craving the shade that never finds us. When the only way out of a desert is to sit with it awhile. Thought we saw the bird flying but in fact it was grounded, lifeless. Drinking sweat from a shirt. The desert a vast, quivering moment, its eyes wide open. In the depths of these uninhabited lands, a bridge over sand ... for what purpose? Scarves failing to filter dust from our lungs. Rubbing eyes with sand-fingers. We travel at night where possible.

zero summer

Sapless days. We should be wasting time,
talked-about! Shamed into games
of silences as we grow older,
our mouths shaping zeroes. But come,

this is an age of prose! So, a
grandiloquent party at the summer palace.
We accept its maze: corridors at random,
the sunroom's dusty vagaries. Morning

decanted through, heat hard
at the windows. Come wrap
the throat of a vase with the blue boa.

Viola music. In the fernery you say
what a pity it is that beauty lifts
so early. Blood beats
upon the underchin and palms.

glitching

want

~ or a rat on rat patrol radar on ~ i'm a business cannot assist i feel
so oh no master of none milky tea on my fingers ~ hired a hand that
couldn't hold ~ the use? ~ finetuned worlds readied to ship ~
slobbed/psy-opped ~ taped mouths ~ taped mouths ~ theft can be
pretty? ~ word-clues snatched into margins ~ don't interfere with
mating plants ~ figured how to decrypt these? ~ secured the bridge
oh flee the inward we spit so much repressed breath ~ pocketed
more face for later ~ gun of a gaze ~ am i raining? ~ quit sleep take
up night ~ fled the junk party room with its pinked haze ~ you want
her nametag though & so many buildings your table not content

moral highchair

saved from that
head over-desiring
the guesswork's
sure unsheer give
'em 3 kilos of ghost
that should be
sufficient how much
they've spent on their
eyes losing like they're
told the dead body
grazed on the bill-
board directed at
drivers overloaded
with i don't knows lost
mission control those
careless astronauts

[? are you a numb]

them glib-feeders crunched debate [? who's first hitter on the team] let's care at least once [? that a glass ain't waterproof] [? whose new look licks] washed our time with don't trouble the radar ask us about lightweight a silken jigsaw done at the day spa [? seduced by precision] the dogbowl filled with toner a sun-enhancer

sleeper

what's said off-air re
dud pills you're not
who they pay you to
be hushing undertow
of riffage tho on alert
for non-imitations as if
deviants make the best
witch-hunters could
you be any more uni

formed & those prods
sting real bad mate
just ask the casual

ties those cartoon
wackies never out

grown a smidge under

dressed for a funeral
the poster boys of neo

tony can only bet on
walkovers tribes of
bacteria colonising
less polite hosts & re
spraypainting the
18th greenskeeper
Jed says he really
has no other option

greyscale

another strobed ascension ties up the air,
    the sky shut down for search ...

an amateur's blurred clips from the water-taxi—
    it's hard to glean any colour ...

is that supposed to be blood spattered
    on the young girl's lens?

the governor's head shrinks to a stone,
    is yet to sprout a spine ...

will there be no end to the vanity projects?
    ('guilt loves company', indeed ...)

what they considered darkness was in fact innumerable
    veering points of light ...

no buttons inside the elevator—just get in,
    hope for the best ...

nurse your caffe forte, practise talking:
    'it was just curiosity, just research' ...

every amateur hour

some swim beyond
reproach the water
robe the dot
orgs wear any
mud hurled sins
of omission hint
your interest more
talented bestiaries the
further back you
dig obscure lexical
artefacts hop out
of freshly minted
tomes to applause
our eyes snacking
on arcs aerodynamic
or otherwise such
a dulled integrity
of suppressed intent
(seldom smiling with
the whole body)

wasted

deleted scenes

ignore what was said while high /
especially with regard to moneys

*

we half-met at the party / so
rude of me (gushy, *italicised*?)

*

<—reverse thrust (er ...)
re-entry anx / sedation

*

damn suspect eyes / the
parents not so naive

*

a total lack / while peaking ...
too much (nothing) to notate

sunday

caught in so much daylight
(plainclothesman's funnel)

skin warmed by the eye
ignored by the hand

limp handshaking all that bridges us
(or else sunday cough)

analog clock semaphores
(calc the time left)

a side-reality sleep deletes
recovered, regeared for travel

pool of glass
under blue light

& were you on an illicit?
your pupils played bent little notes

all the pixels spilled ...

last night city
held words

now that city is missing

meds

Piercing blister foil with thumbnail. Those who call them meds generally those who take them (target group). As if a pill might mainstream you. Conditioned air.

*

Body became a fist, clenched. Having no designated evacuation assembly point. If resistance alone is real. Tension of the oral.

*

Pharmaceutical packaging design says what about what? Bring colour. Cropped Riviera panorama. Starter pack (like life is a series of hobbies).

*

Had never been held by a cloud before. Perennial tremor. A little blur. Doesn't fit in the eye.

*

The white coats only prepared to discuss rituals of personal sanitation in light of the overarching norm. They think they own white light. Smudge that. Gaze predicated on someone's plotline of progress.

*

In need of new plottings, new flows. Medicated for fear of the phone. There is something necromantic. Hi, I'm fine.

*

Recalibrating one's categories of silence. Silence can mean anything but. Slight decoherence. Are you feeling?

*

Lensed into this? Consider the implications of 'appetite alterant'. Of appetite. What is burnt to milk a glow.

*

Entering that hummingbird space. Getting to know those stranded outside the fifteenth wall. Wet with voices. Not possessing that movement.

*

Agonists, all. Neurotransmitter pool. Disinhibitor set him on a biting spree. The two photos show him before and after science.

*

Shipped or funnelled back to consensus reality. Homecoming of sorts, arms open like clouds. A bath of wool. How to be welcome.

virus
(for Kat / props to Laurent Garnier)

techno is/techno is a virus throbbing
   munt-fodder glob stacker
   tractions bluffer venom jugger
   null compressor den richter
   scaled disturbor bots nicer
   loosed repeater stunblaster iris
 airlocks flooded spectrum gridshifts
glasstooth grinder misfitter stealth
 exhibit randometer spectre pulse-flare
   omicron-wasp fluid accelerant blissed-on
   spitter madcap courtships culted brinks
   cursives the roid belt unelected void
    shirkers strewn planetfall peak icebreak
    nano-roboscopic lifter phantasma
    grabby bloater carbonate blunted
     mined dark-end quicksilvery bloodline
    spewer cloned samsara salad flak

post-

late morning   hung-
  over meditation

used the night (smoking
                ghost-dust)

a pearl
   melted in wine

to risk   the beautiful

(landing in
   paracetamol)

now look yourself up: deedless

words asleep, day-
   waste/narrowcast

eyes stung   (fingertip smokestain)

a woman knocks, her
  body a shop?   (not in your wildest)

aviator shades're charms
  to ward off nothing

brain-flies   leave graffiti

that dead-
  cell ache

outrovert

'there is much to keep silent about'

*

that serial mic-in-mouth dream:
hardbodies mass,
your book-smarts
amount to nothing

*

the morning mopes,
hardly good smoking weather

*

a status bar worms
cross-screen
to little purpose

*

timepoor breakfast
eaten off a mirror

*

fast-acting cap
slows the room
to baseline

*

you practise your dice-rolls

but there's no
need to undress
that billboard girl

('she only ever loves a warrior')

psychopathologies

you may
be another:

on-screen
your reflection

homuncular,
an alien

*

clocktime mocks
a drift to war

this insomniac
data hunger

overfocus &
air hockey

*

whose handwriting
is this?

*meditation
is boring*

(thanks
for the intel)

*

without permission
without pretext

data sneezed
into the outer

(memory talks
too much)

*

backslapping
as gloved insult?

reading a dictionary
of symptoms

begin to doubt
your presence in the house

melt

green dust lit in the candle-garden / bending low

into new sproutings, abruptings / how soil

heats, vapour lifts to bridge clouds / thinking

through ownership of the sun / (the sun

that raised me still owns me?) / thinking

to part a heavy curtain / (these windows

will melt away in the end?) / no

end (& then only midways) / only dreams

of a dead androgyne / define yourself

here / identify yourself, strangely

enough / while drinking earthy river-

water / come clean,

whose hallucinations are these?

md & k

half-lit in Tastelounge to remain
undetectable we sit in black
saucers asking each new set of
pupils 'who're you flying with?'

answer: 'Michael Douglas', which
must be drug-code or some such
subception the VJ fastforwards
80s videocassette *How to
Powerwalk* we half-nod to
fluro headbands leggings
strutting the plasmas all

conspires to stream a place
we didn't know we had the
fiction effect our streaky gaze-
coordinates get realmed the

quasi-jungle mazes dance matter
out of place skulled bassheads
wild it out intercorporeal no
nostalgia for the future's the
condensation point wherever
beats're aware of themselves
underlayers form a derm &

atomshake the realm of hungry
ghosts desire sells desire our
needlethroats our tongues
extra pennants of the hex

impair

this head   of
   hiss-trails

will never believe
   the sky   again

this deadhouse
     is   vorpal

words frag up,   walls fuzz

luck = picking up
      a   discard

snorting failsafe
     through $5   bill

how to edge   lost   & safe?

this entertainment hunt's
      not   it

desist
(after Stan Brakhage's *desistfilm*)

the night (is it night?) is
teeth,
sitting around dumbing stuff
we have cool haircuts
if this is the 50s,
sexes thrown in darkroom
music loud enough that we can't

music through a glass, a fly

boredom sits
reading your shoe
tugging our own hairs

surface-bound
sit around dumbing stuff
starting cigarettes
stacking house of books,
his shortlived match sculpture

later run out
screaming deaf into treescraped
horizons, bracken
slow our flame
descend to
magnified touch

at some point back in the room
caught ourselves paused
dancing it was kindergarten
plus an ashtray

our flesh-blur
    strung
     refused that kiss

slippages (undead)

of how things stand:
butcher's window display,
blood residue on pseudo-grass

*

bystander effect:
knowing only the known body,
warding spells, the craven info

*

the skin is not on the map,
acts like it doesn't
want to be here

*

the text-fatigued
the soundproofed
the portable ghost-head

*

camouflage for dread:
rare pills (small gods)
slip blood to the tongue

*

riot police
slur syllables
behind their shield-wall

*

the forced door, systems
breached, direct sun
upon data crypt

*

scared to show the volume
you carry (some sacred relic),
you nest it in your hands

couplings

coupling

who's impersonating who
here / who's mindblowing

who (she too
is edgy / & interior

/ late-night
drip-crack /

a half-pout / making
eyes at no-one

/ he's so hard
to prise / back

turned / to
the landscape / *what*

a couple / part
business part unfinished i.e.

no pash / or words / to that
/ buying what? future

hedges & trades (they
ride within / the system

dote

the night-oath milked
                    from a ballpoint wound

              her carnelian pendant
a battle piece

through a crack in the wifi
                        she refutes his cigarette

                        his loose hunger
to blaze in some hermetic car

how his daily body
                    spilled together

                    within the dropzone
another city cube

walls cratered
                    doors porous as felt

          bedroom a paper clock
on a lilo

rumour rests on a smile
                        like the new maid

              hour by hour
he becomes food

from 'suite (sour remix)'
(for/after Dana Guthrie Martin)

the last dream we :: sit
in a café noise :: of china,
knives :: the too-loud ::
music and rival :: talk at
other :: tables you place
:: your cup over :: your
mouth :: a semi-mask :: I
fence my :: eyes with a ::
napkin and :: the waiter
softly :: asking us to leave

futures

tame

Those who frequent only the indies, the micros. Boycott of giants (armadas of battleships unable to turn). How many m^3 of grey? Crime scene cluster: bank, supermarket, exchange. 'Do not buy my child a gun'.

*

Go bush. Firetraps on the fringes. Generalised iffiness. Network outage the cause? Emergent distraction industries; the simian cornered. Obsolescence inbuilt in all … all are revolving doors. How turning circles tighten. Taming ≠ repair.

*

Unplug these futures. Are we 'headed'? Facer, tone up your voice. Read the insane. Artist seeks oversize mirror? Caffeine a permuter? Adjusting the gain. Eating whatever falls from the sky. Insects fly through rain, never struck by a drop.

the national conversation

Walled by packaging. They don't know how else to function. City at sea. Aromas of coffee and oranges, maybe—but aren't these purely 'for effect'? They skipped through quarantine in their white skin, talking of wealth protection schemes. Mismanagerialism of 'Australia'. The seekers, the thrillseekers, and the marketing flacks. Bio-markers of legal tender. Send in the loans.

*

There seems to be no way of unwrapping this 'gift'. They are unprepared for silence. A city far to the right of its people. Pockmarked from an early case of smallpox, perhaps. The most virulent strains lie dormant in the backyard. The search item 'Australia' was not found. The power tools, the robocalling, and the killswitch. Bio-markers of astral fallout. Send in the clones.

otherwise

wants a new form

formation
of what might be termed 'ungrounded grounds'

... further heterotopias?

here we are, suffering in language

error of taking the dominant for the universal

other crossings being possible?

what's the wild boar so
wild about, after all?

& what counts as
food, as sex, to this tribe?

where the system is vulnerable, wearing
protective gloves while sniffing fruit

corpse with limited functionality: false,
but not only false

the university a department store

fearful of positivities, of being 'taken in',
but and and but

as if Rome might ready itself for such a fall,
reach agreement on the mourning process

it is no doubt forbidden to take
shots of these waste-grounds

miasma (persuasions, dissuasions)

'we see no connection' quips congressman
to network foreign correspondent

once you're talking on this channel you
no longer know what you're talking about

things were about to get physical, then
he hung up

have you a war name?

an instability commutes to another code-zone

departures, arrivals

Airport of the future. Devoid of take-offs, landings. Derelict hub. The passenger era having followed the strip-lights to the exit. Heat of steel, glass. Kids barefoot on tarmac. The encampments were quick to spread here. Spaces once open. Signs no longer apply. Former meanings, functions. Arrows lead to nothings, nowheres. Proliferation of tents, tarps, improvs on a theme of shelter. 'Temporary' uttered less and less (palliative word). Fires throw the only night-lighting. The thinning. Safeties, sanitations (relativities). Sustenance amounts to sprouts in water. Seeds once saved. Harvesting water from the slants of roofs. A hangar become hothouse, an airliner become home. Hierarchies trampled (what of hierarchies of need, triage?) Travel is but a story. The endless elsewhere. What was once a city's most complex intersection (flightpath web). That ancient theme of waiting.

midways

refuse

A day under repair. Unable to stand after meditating (my foot dead as a book). Trying to type but the window was ghosted. Coming down with something: perhaps a poem. My turn to call? Half-life: transactions blur between us; signal fray. Go through phases, moods, like some old moon. Naming will not keep pace. Downloading Derrida. I looked the instant it ticked over. Have a tic about time. Distraction blizzards. Dwelling in the centre of your palm. You've lost me. Cherry-fingers blemish the page. A guilt that grows back. Comedown. Log out, log back in again. Need to work back late, keep watch till dawn. As markets cloud. Remove nothing from the scene of the theft. Where dying is a slowness. Emissions. Heavy myself with. Punjabi pop music strays from another apartment, as if dappling me with glows. I wasn't quite full. Was deleting old songs. The crouched hand of love (from a song of Creeley's). New window. Wheeling towards stories of failures. Driver error. Lab rats in lab coats? They were subtitles for a different film altogether. Photograph these powers of persuasion. But does he look happy to you? Wasting berserker-bots in Timezone. Heroic dopamine leak. Doctor suggests closing both eyes. Hyperrealism of hi-definition. Have fun with it? Sad snaps. Exit the bed via the usual exit. Bivouac: *noun*; an encampment made with tents or improvised shelters, without protection from enemy fire. Have overslept. Just one more snooze before we assemble. Another day speechless, the mouth a lock. Away from the meat. Touch of the air, air of the touch. Refused endings. Everything's not you in one sense, but in another: come home. Swim your body for the first time. Untie these roads and lift them from you.

a book of buddhist monks

A monk tells a story that becomes more and more simple (it is the story of his life).

*

While meditating, a tear flushes the monk's eye.

*

The monk of legend levitates through mist, descends to sit upon another mountain.

*

One monk says meditation means making many starts, until such starting ceases.

*

This monk folds and unfolds his attention, scouts beginnings and ends of desire.

*

Shockproof monk.

*

The first scent of night-flowering jasmine marks the end of the monk's walking meditation.

*

A monk fills the dhamma hall with the clearing of his throat.

*

A nun who was once a monk.

*

That monk appears to have great patience, does not seem to tire of waiting—perhaps he is not waiting at all?

*

A monk falling out of a tree.

clair

the eye that sees clearly
is closed

not dutifully
scanning the news

leaving open-eyed sleep
to the fish

on a sunday slow
with patience

loving those
bird-formations

this barefoot
dance

these tiny
inaccuracies

seven concentrations

1. entrance

This should be easy to enter, like a public building. Not that all public buildings *are* easy to enter, but the idea that they could (or should?) be. 'The complexity of philosophy is not in its subject matter, but in our knotted understanding.' Ha!

2. retreat

'Philosophy unties the knots in our thinking', not unlike a holiday that includes not a single digital component. Our thinking became less mushy once we exited the city. For a moment our bodies felt lighter than notions. A tingling of safety. But ads gave chase, behaving as do subatomic particles, which the physicist can only know by inference. They surfaced even in the most private of spaces: the pimples of the tongue, the shield of the retina. There was no longer a question of where—therefore escape held no meaning. There were arguments already and we needed other channels, other forms of conversation and exchange to emerge.

3. reading

No amount of reading will ever be 'enough'. This does not require a diagram.

4. coding

It wasn't the effect I wanted; this made me especially happy. Inelegant code. Widely-circulated propaganda: shots of webs supposedly threaded by spiders in various states of intoxication.

5. mythology

Overheard: ' … your money where your myth is.' The study of contemporary mythography. Where data ends, where we begin … to feel … unspoken? We can only hope.

6. art

Someone is saying there are too many artists (moths) at this *soirée*. That their code *is* elegant. Pretty in black, sloganesque. To be one of them, one of theirs. Shaping beyond the expected *and* the expectation of the unexpected.

7. meditation

We take smoke-roads out of town, until we rise from morning meditation. A doubt: were we meditating this time, or waiting? To think is to stray. Slipped and cut. The mind, overcharged, wades in all the gone and unwritten. But to return to the point … return after return is the practice. Returning to the one point is the practice.

self-help

a nest is a gathering (opportunity point)

less an escape than a hiding (hiding centres the body)

a morning for lingering (no one is waiting)

pushing the bike uphill (no, the day not in shreds)

reversing that wheel, the eye (stir a little p.m. into the a.m.)

as if you could open anything, seed anything (the Xanax beginning to
 sprout)

how to differ (trembling to the point of weightlessness)

limiting yourself to a certain era (ease outward: other rooms)

to act a tad skylike (become a believer in birds)

orchid dormant (how to make a robe of it?)

inertia's home (or a buddha, a noon point)

waterclock
(remembering John Cage)

catching the overlap,
fragments of water/fragments of sound
generous in their incompleteness

*

land's a slower ocean
& we, too, are trees,
standing on one leg in ecstasy

*

the rain, no longer falling
on anything whatsoever, persists
falling through space

nightside
(a cento for/after Jill Jones)

hours may not be to scale
as when there becomes
here & stars reach

output's end the stadium
birds equally bluffed
by meteorology could you

understand breath
as a casting of doubt
now the bottle's hardly

night-deep a river city's
water moon pretends
to purity where water's

a pilgrimage the gods
look a lot like clouds
stranded without motive

positive poem

up

lit, possible

(largely) undistracted

spring shaping
          (to be scintillant)

nothing to delete

flows

Knowing there would be some way to continue. So many forms of breathing (breath-forms), the many stations of the breath. Breath circuit.

*

Bonding in the spiraling. Breathing changes what happens. Confidence in uniqueness. Trying to find out what the words want. The breathwork.

*

And then you know you're in the detail; glints of the not-yet settle. Let the breath itself do the breathing. Countless forms of yes; yes-forms.

*

Time may enter or be entered ... as flows. Tending toward multiplicity, multiple vectors, multiple persons. Two people will breathe this differently. A close reading of breath ... a close dissolving.

*

Unbounded breath; no beginning, no endpoint of. No bounded system. A house of breath is built and built ... Mind is part of the air.

soil

city soil

Sky-loss. Tower glass self-reflects. We weren't sure where we were. City loses us for a moment.
Oldfangled causes, like darkness. With the ease of abstractions, crowned 'scrapers drift into flaky heavens. Dashing out-of-doors, freshed by a blast of air. Wearing a yellow post-it.

How to be an appearance. Look wildfire. Or look careful-ish. Look an expert faller.
The act of self-composting. But here? Toggle dumps. Level up, level down.

It is the mouth that strives for order; speaking solely in quotations (the questionless). 'Until we know what caused this incident. We can't be certain. It won't recur.'
City & colour. Know this as sepia-grey. The talk of those convincing themselves they like to be caged. How to pick tourists from sly photographers & the choppers banking over-head.

Excess sweat of narrative. Abandoned bike locks still clamped at the foot of steel arches. Lock the ground. Metallic subsoils, plastics, asphalt dunes.
'Thank you for your patience while we build you.' Papery face. The familiar forms a family, the outward. Wife pointing out cute little booties.

Pretending to rain again. Then this path, formed by feet. Site of a former dance-temple. Signs mark distances to houses of breath.
Fined for piffing organic matter. Peel & core. Layer of eggshell from the protests. Partly fused.

City as community garden, cutting across the verticals. Streets &
streets edible, delible. Plucking basil. Turning the sign around.

                                                                The

approachable.

vectors

Water on
stone,
          water
in stone.

*

Vapour-ascension,
          cloudscape &
                    rain.

*

Curvatures of leaf,
          petal
form the watercourse.

*

Seed-time:
          seeds rain wider, wider.

*

Forest of messengers.

*

Traffickings &
          filterings
of light; webbings
          of waveforms.

*

No one moment
 or movement
 prevails.

*

Canopy over ferns
 over soil:
 shadow
upon shadow.

morn

bent grass morning tardy
dew on the garlic olfactory
& tactile pathways bitter-

damp vegetation dispersed
rain-logic a stuttering
knowledge taking

a bypath the birds
sing mappings the fract-
ed foliage there is a

there of bridgings the
homeless mind leaf-
clusters riding ridge-

currents a momentary
scanning pattern a
fielding that stranges

apropos (celebration instructions remix)
(for/after Michael Farrell)

1.

relation between exposure
& strength: poppies touch
it

   to the point of no hands

2.

sunflowers not anchored
by old coins

        to make
art their invisible

3.

insect vision a
nonblind blind

        their
treasure buzz

4.

celebration of husks

5.

the rain-
framed germination
clock

    not the seed
instructions

6.

electric grains

            soft
spools of
early seedlings
purple with the dark

entheogen

fractalina

Ants crawl the beach, distributing
data. Sand drifts into patterns:
ripples, cusps. Sand-waves, sea-
dunes. The vast. Sun surging
amber/violet. Scapes of cloud,
smudging, shaping analogues

of lifeforms. Fractals of
your face ... your circuitries.
Chemical morning; sleep-
deprived, I rest in
your pulse; vistas scroll
over your skin. These layers

and layers. Imagined
and after-image: busy mandalas
bend the spectrum. No linearities,
no wrestling with a cloud. Letting
go into patterning. Footprints on
sand ... or footprints of sand ... ?

latent spacejunk

'In miniscule natural quantities, it's the fuel of fantasy, dreams and visions. The alien-ness of many of the realms of DMT is striking.'
— Robert Hunter

onset: blue overdose / baby
entropies / timelapse / warps
to white-speed / neural flare /
bloodlit behind closed eyes / a
bass drone / buzzing anti-music
/ visible static / insectoid with
UV eyes / wingspan snipping
the winds / the latest creatures
/ prankish henchmen / file in &
out of the dreamt / mutagenic
alien warez / receptor sites / tilt
over into infovore geekery / the
tracer's outcry held back / skulls
of dead techs / 'any crew?' / 'er,
negative.' / words islanded in
midair / give off ghosted light,
encrypt ways home / how to
scroll earthward again / & thaw

music may be older than language

Recursions. Glitching stars tap out the spectrum.
Trees bend fractal. Ventriloquist froglife. Dub-
pond & thicket. Spiralling through. Halt at the
fire to be its student.

Fire lifts, farewells. Night masquerade: some
of the women stand winged; men wear their
animal. Plant-eaters. Shamanic bass. En-
theogen shaving story-layers.

Cosmologies, soteriologies. The death
side. n, n dimethyltryptamine hyper-
space. Discarnate remedy. *Pharma-
kon.* (Dis)enchantress.

An audience with. Far space, upper
time. House of the elders. Inter-
section. Coming to. Drums
begin.

entheogen

Drug as text, as intertext. Prayer without word. Asleep but restless, raiding the fossils. The rise of skin. Distraction room. A temporary language.

Working at that, performing circles. Giving your ghost back (to ...) (to whom?) (to what?) Culturally devalued sphere of goalless activity (art of doing nothing with nothing). What masquerades as getting spaced at a shindig is no less a ritualised enactment of the rupture, the de-rupturing.

Unstitch, sidereal. His eyes were everywhere; her eyes were on. The one that asks, 'Who do you serve?' Utopian move, reading the whole thing at once (an experience misconstrued as 'original' and without history). Series of re-entries. Clowning, eating a spoon.

Not of substance but of form. To paraphrase a sky, the skyed. The markings, the traceries. What holds. Slow spell. Neoned, plaited through time.

cartouche (sands of the desert remix)
(for/after Kristen Bissaillon)

Hard to get off the roads; to abdicate, tread a bypath. Hyper-
naming homeworld. Even *Voyager 1* ferries
hieroglyphs. *Turntables link sun*

and sun. Departing the heliosphere. Lose
your own face for days: an antidote. Words no longer
family. Become aerial, chaos-bait. Palpate

frequencies, patterns heard in pattern-
less. What sun scries. To hereby
mouth the impossible. Heat

travelled. Desert compass an
encumbrance, tarnished silver reflector.
Here the tomb-wastes, ground and sky of

once-flowing city. Remnants of
Ozymandias's amusement. Shadow-
found. Drifts of laughter coiling sands.

exits

after reverdy
(for Paul)

these are false portals
    through which nothing leaves

& what is the endless wall?
    what is the heavy house that sleeps?

a seedsman's garden

    overcrowding of seeds, rose dust

if hope has no object, what are seedlings?

    the garden birds' wings too short for the task

the optimist

Everyone became famous 15 minutes ago.

We are all together in one big tent.

Kittens raised in the dark will never develop normal vision.

'When enough of them are wrong, they're right.'

Children taught the wrong words for everything.

Try pointing towards the undefined.

Suggestible students tend to believe they have whatever disorder
they're currently studying.

'Beyond a certain point, complexity is fraud.'

Final week of the semester: a thinly attended, token lecture on
poetry.

When bored, the monkeys would just masturbate all day.

Losing the ability to say 'I'.

I have always been a wretched speaker.

This tapped fuel source may not prove relocatable.

Like a philosopher, placing everything in inverted commas.

I'm not a fucking mindreader.

Laughter as the 'false-alarm call', revoking the need for assistance.

'If you're not reading this for pleasure, you're not reading it at all.'

Dropping dead from lack of contact.

Window-glass flexed by the wind.

Palm resting on the hump of the mouse.

Going without for months.

Holding pattern.

Short course on how to say 'No'.

Figures you're cute, feels he's getting warm, looks for an entrance.

Primates will signal the location of food.

Overly generic comforting gestures trivialise the extent of the other's sadness.

Whose bullshit detector?

'Have eyes to wonder, but lack tongues to praise.'

'Yay, urban-life technologies warp the psyche in unexpected ways.'

The simplest phrases have their difficulties.

Such gadgets and tripwires seem the preserves of a younger man.

At one time considered becoming a monk, as a path away from distractions.

'The technologist produces a poem, whereas the poet trashes a machine.'

I have never been drunk in my life.

Come on you little shit, everyone's waiting for you.

The first drawing ever produced by an ape was a drawing of the bars of its cage.

Those hoodied block-boys shouting, 'To hell with being awake!'

When sleep deprivation disinhibits.

Ferment.

'Genuine public debate.'

How free can a market be?

The technology ticking flawlessly!

Rampant hyper-deference.

'Sub-par finishing proved the difference.'

Chained to the edit.

Let nothing go unreplied.

rims

I cannot read this memory:
the sky appearing to move
falling like a face
(the sky appearing to move
falling like a face
is at the edge of this)

By way of finishing the thought
an uncertain point
most relevant:
(an uncertain point
most relevant:
the sky appearing to move)

Interpreting the inside:
an insertion
cannot be unmade
(an insertion
cannot be unmade
is at the edge of this)

Looking down from the roof of the capital
the land is thin:
go into any house
(the land is thin:
go into any house
interpreting the inside)

Wading on
the rim of night:
writing returns
(the rim of night:
writing returns
looking down from the roof of the capital)

Limbs of plants in water:
plants at their limits:
I cannot say what they do
(plants at their limits:
I cannot say what they do:
wading on)

Each stood amongst the others' decrees
unable to leave the airport
no one knows the other:
(unable to leave the airport
no one knows the other:
limbs of plants in water)

Of a moth-trap
a wrongful place:
to wriggle free
(a wrongful place:
to wriggle free
each stood amongst the others' decrees)

By way of finishing the thought
because it is in the past:
the self a convenient example
(because it is in the past:
the self a convenient example
of a moth-trap)

a dead boy

the river is lost

the flowers dry
and fulvous

shards of cold glass in the bed
for which you are now too tall

the pale bird in the tree
is made of paper

the tree is made of paper
and green glass

another dust-wave
climbs away from earth

here where you are sleeping

poem

no signal, no receiver

*

perhaps only a god

*

for those still in play, a need
to know where your dead are buried

*

'showing no fear'
(a displacement)

*

lay a stream here

notes

amor fati: 'Begin anywhere' is a saying attributed to John Cage.

outrovert: This poem begins and ends with lines ('there is much to keep silent about' and 'she only ever loves a warrior') from Friedrich Nietzsche's *On the Genealogy of Morals*, translated by Douglas Smith, Oxford University Press, 1997.

desist: After Stan Brakhage's short film, *desistfilm* (1954).

from suite (sour remix): An excerpt from a remix of Dana Guthrie Martin's poem 'One Seed: Persephone's Suite'. Dana's poem was published in *The Spare Room*, Blood Pudding Press, 2009. The book is now out of print, but can be read online here: http://issuu.com/danaguthriemartin/docs/the_spare_room.

refuse: 'The crouched hand of love (from a song of Creeley's)' refers to Robert Creeley's poem 'Love' (first line: 'Not enough. The question: what is.') in *Selected Poems*, University of California Press, 1991.

seven concentrations: 'The complexity of philosophy is not in its subject matter, but in our knotted understanding' and 'Philosophy unties the knots in our thinking' are remarks by Ludwig Wittgenstein, as quoted by Anthony Kenny in *Wittgenstein*, Allen Lane, 1973.

waterclock: This poem was prompted by (and draws upon for some words and phrases) the following books: John Cage, *M: Writings '67-'72*, Wesleyan, 1973; John Cage and Joan Retallack, *Musicage*, Wesleyan, 1996; John Cage and Daniel Charles, *For the Birds*, Marion Boyers, 2000; Richard Kostelanetz, *John Cage*, Allen Lane, 1974.

nightside: A cento, containing some words and phrases from Jill Jones's book *Dark Bright Doors*, Wakefield Press, 2010.

apropos (celebration instructions remix): After Michael Farrell's poem 'apropos', published in *Open Sesame*, Giramondo, 2012.

latent spacejunk: The epigraph (a Robert Hunter quote) appears in a dialogue available here:
http://www.levity.com/orfeo/index.part1.html

cartouche (sands of the desert remix): After Kristen Bissaillon's poem 'cartouche'. The words *'Turntables link sun and sun'* appear in her poem, which can be viewed here:
http://1figure.blogspot.com.au/2008/01/cartouche.html.

the optimist: Parts of this poem were prompted by Alice Flaherty's book *The Midnight Disease* (Mariner Books, 2005), and a 1962 BBC Television interview with Vladimir Nabokov, the transcript of which is available here:
http://www.lib.ru/NABOKOW/Inter02.txt_with-big-pictures.html.
'Have eyes to wonder, but lack tongues to praise': Shakespeare, from Sonnet 106.

publication credits

Versions of poems in this collection have previously appeared in the following publications (Australian unless noted):

The Best Australian Poems 2012: 'the 6-star experience'.

Cordite: 'syd', 'apropos (celebration instructions remix)', 'rims'.

Counterexample Poetics (US): 'every amateur hour'.

fourW: 'a book of buddhist monks'.

Journal of Interdimensional Poetry (US): 'latent spacejunk', 'music may be older than language'.

Leaves Literary Journal: 'outrovert', 'self-help', 'flows', 'sands', 'fractalina', 'after reverdy'.

Lit Up (US): 'bud'.

madswirl (US): 'sunday'.

Otoliths: 'amor fati', 'art in the age of digital reproduction', 'amsterdam', 'want', 'moral highchair', '[? are you a numb]', 'virus', 'md & k', 'the national conversation', 'otherwise', 'seven concentrations'.

Overland: 'departures, arrivals'.

PASH capsule: 'coupling', excerpt from 'suite (sour remix)'.

Rabbit: 'avignon', 'psychopathologies'.

Sein und Werden (UK): 'desist'.

Small Wonder: an anthology of prose poems & microfiction: 'meds', 'refuse'.

Stoned Crows & other Australian icons: 'down south'.

VLAK (Czech Republic): 'art in the age of digital reproduction', 'weft', 'city soil', 'entheogen'.

Windmills: 'zero summer', 'slippages (undead)', 'waterclock', 'a dead boy'.

Wordly: 'self-help', 'after reverdy'.

www.ingramcontent.com/pod-product-compliance
Lightning Source LLC
Chambersburg PA
CBHW052119090426
42741CB00009B/1872